# ON AMBIVALENCE

# ON AMBIVALENCE

The Problems and Pleasures of
Having It Both Ways

Kenneth Weisbrode

The MIT Press

Cambridge, Massachusetts

London, England

MIT Press books may be purchased at special quantity discounts for business or sales promotional use. For information, please email special_sales@mitpress.mit.edu or write to Special Sales Department, The MIT Press, 55 Hayward Street, Cambridge, MA 02142.

This book was set in Adobe Garamond and Gotham by The MIT Press. Printed and bound in the United States of America.

Library of Congress Cataloging-in-Publication Data

Weisbrode, Kenneth.

  On ambivalence : the problems and pleasures of having it both ways / Kenneth Weisbrode.

    p. cm.

    ISBN 978-0-262-01731-2 (hardcover : alk. paper) 1. Ambivalence. 2. Decision making. 3. Choice (Psychology) I. Title.

  BF575.A45W455 2012

  128'.4—dc23

                          2011031303

10  9  8  7  6  5  4  3  2

# Contents

Masolino da Panicale, *The Temptation of Adam and Eve*, c. 1425, Brancacci Chapel, Santa Maria del Carmine, Florence.

It began with Adam and Eve. Do we or don't we eat the apple? "Why not?" says Eve. "Why?" wonders Adam. They chose, half-heartedly, and nothing was ever the same again.

This is a guide to thinking about the condition of ambivalence in the present moment. It is a condition worse than most because it can lead to catastrophe. It is so ubiquitous that many people accept it as normal, and blur the difference between "yes" and "no." Making a choice gives one a fifty percent chance of being right. Ambivalence would seem to give one a one hundred percent chance of losing out. So why do we persist in it?

Ambivalence lies at the core of who we are. It is something more subtle, and more devastating, than human frailty. Weaknesses can be remedied. Ambivalence comes, rather, from too much ambition. Desire begets dissatisfaction, and vice versa. Optimization becomes a fetish. Wanting the "best" means that we must have *both* or even *all* and are reluctant to give up *any* option lest we pull up the roots of our desire. That is why ambivalence is so hard to confront, understand, or master. And why it can be so disastrous.

Most of us know this. Yet we continue to deny it.

I

One of the first manifestations of ambivalent behavior for many of us is with appetite. Do I really want that extra piece of pie? Do I need that diamond ring? Of course we want these things. At the same time we do not, or some part of our selves we call our conscience gives us second thoughts, which appear in the form of a contradiction: No, I don't really want or need that. So the most basic type of ambivalence originates with desire, namely in the contradiction between the heart and the head. At some point, the question of Do I or don't I *want* then becomes one of Do I or don't I *do*.

Between wanting and doing—desire and action—lies ambivalence. It joins doubt with confinement, appetite with volition, while at the same time dividing them from one another, and from their opposites, in practice.

The solution is almost never to gain more options: it is impossible to divide something into three halves. Nor can ambivalence be solved by merging elements of options A and B, in part because most dualities are false. Cyril Connolly, the writer and editor, warned of this: there are no pure opposites, nor is there a happy medium between male and female, ideal and real, reason and instinct, mind and matter, attraction and repulsion, hope and fear, Whig and Tory, stoic and epicurean, yin and yang and all the rest. "The river of truth," he concluded, "is always splitting up into arms that reunite. Islanded between them the inhabitants argue for a lifetime as to which is the mainstream." Connolly, one of his generation's most astute critics, never wrote a real book of his own, never able or willing to concentrate his formidable mind on a single subject. His writings are little more than a sublime pastiche: testament to a frustrated and fragmented self, stuck between the infinite capacity for appreciation and the finite measure of inadequacy, as though a superhuman power of hearing made one a mute. Such are the ideals of consumption and production: it is impossible to achieve complete success in both.

In the world of our imaginations, however, dualities and polarities persist. Ambivalent characters are among the best-known in popular lore. Adam and Eve begot the warring

Cain and Abel; Abraham deliberated over the fate of his son Isaac; Isaac in turn was torn between love and duty to his sons Jacob and Esau. The New Testament gave us Mary Magdalene and the passionate contrast of virtue with vice; Pontius Pilate and the double-edged sword of authority over truth and justice; Mark 3:25 ("And if a house is divided against itself, that house will not be able to stand") and Matthew 6:24 ("No one can serve two masters"). There was Chuang Tzu's butterfly, unsure if he was an insect masquerading as a philosopher or the reverse; Kierkegaard's Johannes the Seducer, whose pleasures prefaced a higher form of ethics; Dante's Beatrice and Andrew Marvell's coy mistress, just two examples of the maidens whose superior beauty catapulted them into the realm of the unattainable; Buridan's ass, suspended in a paradox between the satiation of hunger or of thirst; Balzac's Old Goriot, the tragic father whose lucre was turned against him; Hermann Hesse's Narcissus and Goldmund, favorites of generations of struggling adolescents who cling to the impossible freedom of choice between body and mind; Theodor Storm's birds and butterflies, blending the exquisite with the extinct; Schumann's piano works, skating along the boundaries of playfulness and madness, like the drawings of Paul Klee or the early semantic games of Wittgenstein; complexity masquerading as bland simplicity in the "multiforms" of Mark Rothko.

And Hamlet. We think of his dilemma as existential: do I or don't I wish to exist, or perhaps to exist only in a certain way? Hamlet's doubts were really those of status: am I blessed or condemned? A sane person could hardly want both. Hamlet's more immediate dilemma in fact had less to do with his existence than with the exercise of life. "To be or not to be" very often comes down to "to do or not to do," or, more precisely, *what* to do versus what to *do*. Just as watching pennies is supposed to take care of pounds, asking the question in this way would set aside more difficult metaphysical dilemmas. When in doubt, act, even if that means doing nothing.

\*

There exist several varieties of ambivalence. The man who invented the term, Eugen Bleuler, identified three: the love-hate relationship, focused upon a single object; the inability to choose (or to imagine a choice) between desires, or needs; and the simultaneous attachment to incompatible or contradictory ideas, or beliefs. All tend to blur in practice. Moreover they reflect "inner experience," in the words of the sociologist Robert Merton, and have little to do, at least explicitly, with society and with the particular tension between our impulses and the roles society assigns to them. For Merton and others like him (notably Norbert Elias), the resulting sublimation of the multitude by the individual constitutes the essence of ambivalence. It is in our collective behavior, however, that ambivalence perhaps has its greatest impact. It "diffuses" and worsens as it becomes more general or abstract.

Many of the manifestations we see every day—love-hate, passive-aggressive, fight-flight, and so forth—also relate to sex. And so much of ambivalence as we understand it comes from Bleuler's contemporary, Sigmund Freud, who placed it with sex and sexuality at the root of the power of the taboo, or what he called "impulses to perversion," leading to various kinds of repression. Freud's later opponents—Carl Jung and Erich Fromm, for example—tried to square his circle by promoting a male-female archetype meant to signify, perhaps, that living may coexist with dying, that the Freudian life and death instincts need not be so adversarial, and that such coexistence (or cohabitation) need not be a psychological prison. Paradoxes for some can be liberating, especially for those who embrace collective dualities, and for others who embrace suicide instead. One is reminded of Keats, "half in love with easeful Death": about as ambivalent a statement as one could make on the subject. Still to others, like the sociologist Zygmunt Bauman, they comprise the "modern trinity: ambivalence, freedom and skepticism."

Before Freud, ambivalence did not have so many expressions. It was generally associated with hypocrisy; freedom wasn't something many people took for granted; whereas skepticism, according to Bauman, led to madness.

There are additional pre-Freudian meanings. Ancients knew the Pythagorean distinction between the mortal, or bounded, and the infinite, also known as the One and the Many; it later would be symbolized by the figure of the cross. Other, seemingly interchangeable, opposites are revealed in language: "cleave," for instance, means to split apart and also to cling to; the Latin *altus* means both high and deep; some words for white (e.g., *blanc*) share an origin with those for black (Indo-European *bhleg*, meaning to shine or gleam). In noting them, the philosopher Susanne Langer recalled the important intersections of metaphor and experience that evolve diachronically, whereby every primitive concept arises and exists in an area of relevance, ranging from its own logical domain to its converse domain, and including all conceptions lying between these extremes. The roots of language usually convey ideas of felt experience, i.e., either of action or of impact, and feeling is good or bad, pleasant or unpleasant, with a continuum between them, which, taken from either end, somewhere (not necessarily halfway) breaks over into its opposite.

The modern equivalent of this phenomenon may be found in the tension, sometimes creative, between order and disorder, and between the subjective and the objective delimitation of space. The human community struggles to survive, somewhere, in the middle.

Post-Freud, we recognize that ambivalence, as well as certainty, requires volition and awareness: they depend on sanity, even rationality. This means accepting as valid the principle of choice. Peter Berger and Anton Zijderveld, for example, have touted it, alongside doubt, as modernity's great achievement and the necessary "middle ground between religious belief and unbelief on the one hand, and knowledge and ignorance on the other." Wanting both is the same as wanting neither in some cases. But in most, casting doubt as the incubator of choice is a necessary means to an end: human survival.

So far so good, though we detect something of a non sequitur here. There must be, as the two authors later admit, limits to doubt and to volition: praise is not the same as celebration. Indecision likewise is not the same as ambivalence. Indecision can be many things, from mere hesitation to an abundance of caution to timidity or confusion. Indecision may even be, in the satirical words of Ambrose Bierce, "the chief element of success," to wit:

"Your prompt decision to attack," said General Grant on a certain occasion to General Gordon Granger, "was admirable; you had but five minutes to make up your mind in."

"Yes, sir," answered the victorious subordinate, "it is a great thing to know exactly what to do in an emergency. When in doubt whether to attack or retreat I never hesitate a moment—I toss up a copper."

"Do you mean to say that's what you did this time?"

"Yes, General; but for Heaven's sake don't reprimand me: I disobeyed the coin."

Confusing ambivalence with indecision is common, for the obvious reason that it takes as long not to make a decision as it does to make one when we don't want to decide. But indecision comes from a flaw in character; ambivalence is a spiritual condition. Ambivalence is more paralyzing because it combines the inability to choose with the refusal to admit the necessity of choice. It compels more, not less, responsibility for a suboptimal result. An ambivalent person seeks to overstep mortal limitations; an indecisive person is simply unfree.

With modernity came a war upon ambivalence, whereby the collective will supplanted the "lofty resignation" of the ancients. Human beings could, and should, determine their own fate. Truth was knowable both by the one and by the many, not in parallel but organically and interchangeably. The twentieth century saw such faith in human capacities reach an almost absurd extreme, and ambivalence paid a price. There is the story of the eminent philosopher W. V. Quine who, when asked how he could cope with the removal of the key with the question mark from his typewriter—modified for the addition of an obscure symbol of formal logic—answered, "It was easy. I have certainty." Only a modern philosopher could say that.

Postmodernism flipped this on its head. Postmodernism was about consumers, not producers, which has led to the "privatization of ambivalence ... abolishing the choice itself" so that, again according to Bauman, "the great, three-hundred-year modern war against ambivalence is no longer conducted by regular conscript armies, but by guerrilla units coming together and disappearing again in the dark blind alleys which intersperse the brightly lit avenues of the postmodern disneylands of free consumers."

Where does that leave us? It is impossible to say what will emerge from the fragmentation of the collective will, ambivalent or otherwise, in the jetsam of postmodernism. Bauman suggested a possibility with those guerrilla units—only it is probably better to term them neither postmodern nor antimodern but premodern; that is, we seem to have embarked on an apparently—perhaps deceptively—cyclical path back to the mutual sublimation of individual and collective dualities. Perhaps this is a logical feature of an information-saturated culture that at once denies its underlying ambivalence and actively promotes a multiplicity of human choice, as we shall soon see. Freud showed in an earlier context that such paradoxes, or rather pathologies, could eventually lead to social suicide. We might go so far as to term this a meta-ambivalent position: an ambivalence about ambivalence. Tracing the genealogy of ambivalence to this ultimate point in the evolution of human consciousness in turn leads us to question whether and how it has changed in both depth and breadth, and whether it is more typical of characters, especially societies, in seeming decline, that is to say, entities governed by consensus, accommodation, and committees rather than by heroic individuals. But we get ahead of ourselves. First we must revisit a few more of the ways that ambivalence is expressed individually.

II

Back to typologies. In contemplating the lonely individual struggling over what to do and who to be, we turn again to language, which, according to the literary critic William Empson, is frequently, almost universally, ambiguous. He identified seven types of ambiguity. Most touch upon ambivalence. The first, for example, is the "intention to mean several things [and] a probability that one or other or both of two things has been meant," while the third, in similar fashion, is "when two ideas, which are connected only by being both relevant in the context, can be given in one word simultaneously" so that they "tal[k] about one thing and impl[y] several ways of judging or feeling about it"; and so forth.

It is the seventh type—"when two meanings of the word . . . are the two opposite meanings defined by the context, so that the total effect is to show a fundamental division in the writer's mind"—that allowed Empson to invoke Freud and the paradox of satisfaction: the "notion of what you want involves the idea that you have not got it," in other words, "the opposite defined by your context." Here again we see the incompatibility of thought and action, reaffirmed now as primal desire. We cannot have what we want and we want what we cannot have; to want is to lack, and vice versa. In this formulation, one versus both is made equivalent to nothing versus all; each comes to represent the stark choice stated above between the haves and have-nots, with the quantity of options becoming secondary to the act of choice, its execution, and its psychic consequences. To Empson, this was the ambivalence of the quest, at once toward and away from the desired object, as he cited in the story of Jack and the Beanstalk and the lines of George Herbert's poem "The Sacrifice":

O all ye who pass by, behold and see;
Man stole the fruit, but I must climb the tree;
The tree of life to all, but only me:
Was ever grief like mine?

Ambivalence makes us think more of movement than of destination or direction. Whether we go up or down, forward or backward, may not matter as much as how fast or how slow we go, and what we see and do along the way. What we really want seems to be desire itself; or that our desire to want what we cannot have, or more than we can have, is interwoven with fate, much as truth, in Bierce's apropos words, is "an ingenious compound of desirability and appearance." Desire and desirability, once again, are the basis of ambivalence, just as the appearance and reality of desire, the object and the idea of the object, beat almost indistinguishably in the human heart.

There is more to this than a flawed but inescapable tension of opposites. We may also recall the binaries of Claude Lévi-Strauss and the structures they inspired as a kind of linguistic game: to think at the same moment of the thing and its opposite forces us to devise a language to mediate them, to keep them from turning us all into abject schizophrenics. The structures of mediation perform as an inhibitor cell in the social personality: a yellow light that tells us to pause before going forward pell-mell with green, or paralyzing ourselves with red.

Ambivalence may not be so bad after all. Yellow lights do not incapacitate us; they merely help us get where we are going safely. When we slow down we look around, contemplate, and create. The psychiatrist Joost Meerloo described creativity as a device to subject time to our will by stuffing it with fantasies, and reminded us that Janus was originally the god of gates, doors, and new beginnings, as in the month of January. So if "art is memory" and "memory is reenacted desire," then Cyril Connolly was wrong: the ambivalent river of truth need not flow all the way to oblivion.

Getting from here to there can still be torturous. Ambivalence hurts. Life for most of us, sadly, is not a halcyon succession of pauses and new beginnings. And if we do not have a clear image of the destination, we are in for a rough ride. In so conflating the unattainable with the inescapable, ambivalence flies in the face of Time. History is the infamous argument without end because it is as much about the present and future as it is about the past. The ambiguity of time is reflected in the ambivalent meaning of terms like crisis, threshold, sea change, et cetera. All refer to endings as well as beginnings; yet all are "ambivalent in specifying meaning and seeking meaning alike," in historian Reinhart Koselleck's dichotomous proposition, captured in the title of his book, *Futures Past*: it is as much a question of truth as it is one of power. "Mastering the past" means controlling the future. So too is the future an opportunity to control the past. In some ways, that is all the future really is—a way to rewrite and redefine the past in light of the present.

What if we cannot make up our minds about the past? The bifurcation of historical memory has existed since the days of Zeno with the contrast of two selves in time: time as "a continuous flow" versus time as "the sum of different intervals." The latter gives comfort, even joy, so long as it is tied to the familiarity of the present. The former frightens; it becomes, in Meerloo's words, "a sinister infinity." Long ago Kant cast this problem as the vital difference between space and time: our inner sense revolves around our representation of time; our outer sense, of space. But his may be too easy a distinction. Meerloo was right to conflate infinity with eternity.

Does space scare us more than time? Or is the problem simply that some time (understood as space or "empty" time) cannot be filled with what we know and love? The neurotic personality seeks to push the clock forward, "to borrow from the future." It is the *horror vacui*, Meerloo also recalled, that so plagues schizophrenics (another of Bleuler's invented terms, incidentally) who transpose the before and the after. They abhor, pervert, demonize the past.

The *horror vacui* becomes a *horror metaphysicus*—Bauman's "horror of indetermination"—as soon as it becomes clear that death awaits all who live, and vice versa: "it is in dying that we are born to eternal life," as St. Francis's famous prayer concludes a series of Lévi-Strauss-like paradoxes. So, too, the reverse. The existentialists were not the first to correlate life's chaos with assured extinction. "The continuous work of our life," wrote Montaigne, "is to build death." It is easier to know what we flee from than what we seek. Most of us understand this, yet we repress it in favor of living the good life. Doing so, however, is a race against time. We are all human sandcastles. Here lies the temporal solution to the horror—to understand ambivalence as movement toward both life and death, which means to further, and to limit, contain, or resist, decay by embracing it. "Decline in ecstasy!" Meerloo urged, mimicking the voice of the appeaser *in extremis*: "addiction is the apotheosis of ambivalence."

We needn't be Freudians to see how easy it is to depict ambivalence as a basic and unavoidable struggle between life and death. For most of us this is a simple choice; but who can be sure that the suicide artist doesn't also wish to live but finds dying to be a better option for some reason? Hamlet's question was a theoretical one. In the real world many people want both to be and not to be. They want to preserve both options in perpetuity. Yet living a life free of the prospect of death is almost as difficult as the opposite, temporary suicide, which is impossible. So is finding a solution to the problem by fighting it: that is, insisting on having additional options that don't exist.

*

Attitudes toward ambivalence are said to vary as much by space as by time. Nobody can be in two places at once, yet our inner sense of space and place is often divided. The compass contains four principal directions, again like the cross. North, south, east, and west all have cultural—or what some like to describe as civilizational—connotations, yet none are pure. Clive Bell, the art critic, once observed that it is more difficult to know what civilization is than what it is not: "whereas it is pretty generally agreed that certain societies have been civilized, and even highly civilized, there is no such consensus of opinion about persons." His interlocutor replied, "I can't tell you what civilization is, but I can tell you when a state is said to be civilized." Meaning not that civilization and barbarism are necessarily in the eye of the beholder (though for some people they may be), but that the inner and outer senses of being civilized are in competition, dependent as they are upon the subjectivity of any culture that distinguishes itself from any other. Remember that "civilization develops not from Abel," Carl Sagan declared, "but from Cain the murderer." Civilization, like gentility, is therefore under constant threat by the very nature of being known and judged principally by its consumers, not its creators. Bell again: "the essential characteristic of a highly civilized society is not that it is creative, but that it is appreciative." So too with progress. If civilization has a cultural and spiritual center, it is made up of peripheries looking away from themselves, just as sensation in the human body, according to Susanne Langer, results from external stimuli that adapt, respond, and make themselves internal, producing feeling, which then extends outward. "Every symbolic projection," consequently, "is a transformation." The sense of space and place, then, like time, results from an inter-action at once ambivalent and organic.

We may consider Thomas Mann's em-blematic character Tonio Kröger, the child of a stern Teutonic father and a passionate Latin mother who could never feel at home in the North or the South and is forced to move regularly from one to the other, part of him always needing to be elsewhere; or of the East-West bifurcation of certain cultures like the Russian, Turkish, and even Japanese. Scien-tists in Japan, for example, have proposed that the human brain may be the same around the world but that the ways by which it reacts to stimuli differ considerably. "Eastern" brains focus on the background, collectivities, con-texts, while "Western" brains focus on the individual in the foreground. Really? Who can say whether a brain is predominantly one or the other? Surely, to varying degrees, it is both, just as it's impossible to be entirely "left-" or "right-brained." But this doesn't stop us from wondering.

The biodeterministic impulse is not new. Over three decades ago, for example, Sagan traced its appeal from Pliny to Ein-stein in equating the dual structure of the human brain not only with the capacity to dream, to know, and to feel, but also with the mythical expulsion from Eden. "No mat-ter how far apart the beginnings of research in various fields may be," Langer predicted, "their later developments converge, and in advanced stages tend to dovetail, and close like the perfect sutures of our skull, which become well-nigh invisible in old age." Yet the secret sources of ambivalence are unlikely to be revealed fully by neuroscience. So what does it accomplish? Learning about the function of the human brain is fascinating. But should we alter it in some way? Or do we merely obtain from science a perverse pleasure in pinpointing (if we can) the sources of affliction? We sense that there is more to ambivalence than the sum of a few neurological parts; that it is at the root of virtually everything that afflicts us, from indecision to paranoia. Why? Uncovering the sources of ambivalence in the human brain is an ambitious quest for an answer; but like many behavioral adventures, it tends to open (or reopen) another can of worms. Ambivalence surely relates to as many other problems—not least of which is consciousness—as synapses and neurons traverse brain lobes, all in disputation with one another and contesting one another's convictions, but also working in tandem; which is what F. Scott Fitzgerald probably meant when he wrote that "the test of a first-rate intelligence is the ability to hold two opposed ideas in the mind at the same time, and still retain the ability to function."

\*

Many brain-centered explanations resemble the work of behavioral economics—in what one of its most durable practitioners, Thomas Schelling, aptly called "the intimate contest for self-command." In seeking a typology of value, the economist also grapples with unmasterable time and space. "One model suggested for this ambivalence in choice," according to Schelling,

would let the two selves—or the several—differ along a single dimension amenable to economic analysis. That is the dimension of time preference— of the discount rate to compare present with future, near future with far future, imminent with remote, or permanent with transient. The idea is that the person who takes that drink or lights that cigarette or digs into that hot fudge sundae is merely discounting the future with a high interest rate.

The economist surely knows that there is more to ambivalence than a price comparison of sundaes, cigarettes, and bran flakes. The ambivalent soul will probably want all of the above, and more: to enjoy the benefits without the costs; to value and to overcome the luxury of idleness; in other words, to have it both ways. What good is there in assuming otherwise?

Even if there is an empirical answer to the question of choice, and there probably is not, we still have to contend with the old problem of rationality. It is also ambivalent. To deny this is to be hypnotized by the transfer of faith to an objective market, which is to human volition what irony is to fact: an evasion of both acting and doing; in other words, a false ambivalence that parades "value" only from the outside in, rather than as it really happens, by way of desire. This doesn't mean everything is relative or subjective, or that it is not sometimes possible, under certain conditions, as Herbert Simon proposed, to "satisfice"; rather that rationality is never uniform; that there is no single rational outcome that negates the costs of ambivalence, however rational ambivalence itself can be. Even Schumpeter's characterization of capitalism as a process of creative destruction would seem to rest upon a rational foundation. Mutually exclusive choices may be entirely rational, just as wanting a bit of both, or being unable to choose, is also rational.

Now, that may fly in the face of the commonsense definition of ambivalence (and, for that matter, of desire) as basically irrational. A fragmented rationality is not the same thing as its irrational opposite, no matter how many times we change our minds. Introspection and self-criticism are ambivalent activities, but not without reason. A second guess does not overtake its predecessor; it augments it. Life is rarely anything but cumulative—including the accumulation of reversals.

To acknowledge the fragmented rationality of ambivalence is the first step to realizing just how perverse (and irrational) a blind faith in rational choice can appear, even to enthusiasts like Berger and Zijderveld. This is the oft-cited "decision paralysis" in many of the world's richer countries, particularly, so say today's cultural critics, of the "millennium generation." Hundreds of cable television channels, infinite choices for one's attention on the Internet and elsewhere, the ability, indeed the predilection, for "multitasking," in both daily life and social relationships: to be able to communicate simultaneously to multiple people and to commit—that is, to create an exclusive affiliation—to none of them if we choose. Whenever the question "Do you want to do X?" is posed, we can repeat, indiscriminately, to all offers, "I'm not sure, I'll have to see." Each decision to do this may be perfectly rational; the cumulative effect is not. The sum of ambivalent parts almost never amounts to a rational whole.

III

What is to be done about ambivalence? A better question is, what can be done with it? Nobody likes to suffer paralysis, torment, or squandered opportunity. We usually just opt for delay. Conquering ambivalence otherwise requires a choice—and, paradoxically, a renunciation of ambivalence on the macro level by an acceptance of it on the micro level. This cannot be easy.

Having it all also means more shades of gray, and feeding those Bauman called the "inner demons of assimilation." Rather than choosing outright, we hope to find just one more workable alternative, a happy middle ground, a third way—in other words, a compromise. Compromises are never ideal, except occasionally in retrospect. Some are even "rotten," that is, immoral. "Rotten compromises usually are at the heart of darkness," wrote the philosopher Avishai Margalit. He called them simply "inhuman."

Is a rotten compromise really worse than capitulation or no decision at all? Possibly. In some cases they can mean the same thing. "Does compromise always require something like splitting the difference?" Margalit asked. "Not quite. There is a notion that views the essence of compromise not so much in splitting the difference as in the willingness to accept a reconstruction of what is in dispute." Yet morality, or rather an absolute notion of morality, is never completely absent, which is how Margalit distinguished basic compromises from rotten ones. There is such a thing as a lesser evil, even though sometimes it is a figment of our imagination, just as the trompe l'oeil connotes two simultaneous realities: the one we see and the one we sense.

Finding a partial solution to ambivalence not only calls for a deeper understanding of its consequences but also, again, for distinguishing its exercise from its essence. The former varies considerably and may, in some cases, be managed, even overcome. But the latter is permanent. There is not much we can do about it apart from acknowledging and trying to understand it. That is why it is important to distinguish ambivalence's individual and collective consequences, and, *pace* Empson, ambivalence from ambiguity: for as much as the latter may be used to mask the former, the former is not inconsistent with clarity, and may even be helped by it.

*

Some Americans will say that in the Obama era we have come to embrace our dual natures—perhaps with some success individually but with great anxiety as a society. To insist that there is no red America, no blue America, but one America begs definition. What color is it? Must it be any color? Of course it is many, probably innumerable, colors, *e pluribus unum* and all that, but how exactly do we get to one from many? Is there room for ontology in a social kaleidoscope?

Another term for the Obama era may be, simply, the era of ambivalence. Obama himself may appear or sound ambivalent at times, but mainly he seems to be a man of strong convictions. That they are so often "in the middle" in the Solomonic sense speaks to the man's juridical predisposition, which is probably why his putative compromises have tended to frustrate supporters as much as opponents who seem to miss the predictable clarity of America's adversarial tradition. His political method has been the converse of the one made notorious by Bill Clinton: the so-called triangulation that stole the best (i.e., the most popular) positions of his rivals and called them his own. Obama instead looks at all sides, points to an evidently central position that almost nobody has championed, and then challenges every-

one to accept it as the best of all possible so-
lutions, or at least the best that can be found
under the circumstances. One reason this has
worked for him relatively well so far is that
nearly every ideologue has tended to run for
the hills in response, reacting in ever more
"extreme" ways. Amid the shrill cacophony,
Obama has appeared, over and over, as the
deliberative voice of sanity, which seems for
the moment to have appeased the great silent
ambivalent majority. The luckiest politicians
tend to be those with enemies prone to self-
destruction; this has been true for Obama,
which has accentuated his evident talent for
political jujitsu. That it has been a form of
jujitsu which advertises a rational, wise, and
patent centrism seems all the more remark-

able when noting how much it has capital-
ized upon the country's deep ambivalence
about its future while reinforcing, at the same
time, a utopian discourse that translates "I
want" into "I can."

Why has this occurred now? To claim
that we are living in an ambivalent era is
to presuppose the existence of alternatives.
There is one available in Eric Hobsbawm's
*Age of Extremes*, the fourth and last of his
well-known modern histories. One need not
be a Marxist like Hobsbawm to appreciate
that description of the twentieth century,
whether we say it ended in 1989, 1991, 2001,
or even sometime in the late 1970s to the
middle 1980s with the proliferation of the
microchip, the communications satellite, the

personal computer. The twentieth century was full of utopias; it has left us a large bequest of ambivalence. If globalization, then, stands for nothing less than the universal application of *e pluribus unum*, what are we to make of the certainties of time and space in the contemporary world? Surely globalization begets and reinforces ambivalence. Its emphasis, even dependence, on interconnectivity, interchangeability, "hybridity," and so forth leaves many of us with a sense of loss of place, space, and linear time.

This also is not new. Many people in the West felt similarly disrupted, probably even more so, at the turn of the last century when all that seemed solid about the Victorian era melted into air, and when, in the words of T. J.

Jackson Lears, the "process of identity forma-
tion" that "generated ... insoluble conflicts
between autonomy and dependence" finally
broke apart. Or during the last decades of the
eighteenth century, when, according to another historian, Dror Wahrman, ambiguities
in gender and racial identities prompted the
construction of more rigid categories with
the transformation of attributes into norms,
from the "basically mutable" to the "essential
and immutable."

However, in these two latter cases we refer to the experience of only a minority of the
world's population, namely the portion of it
that was engulfed by the "modern," either in
the so-called metropole or in its extensions
into the then colonial world. It is safe to say

that most people on earth were affected only indirectly by modernity in 1900 and therefore not overly disconcerted by it.

This is no longer true. Globalization has merged with universalism: it now means far more than the ability of some individuals (or commodities, ideas, etc.) to circumnavigate and settle the globe; today it engulfs whole societies, in fact, so that most of humanity can be said to possess something resembling a global consciousness. There is now, in other words, the universal realization that there is one planet, in space, on which we all coexist. Precisely when this happened is not as important as realizing how central it is to the condition of ambivalence. For just as a contemporary reflection on where we stand in time conflates memory and history, making us ambivalent about the shape of the latter, a similar reflection on where we stand in the world conflates the proverbial local and global, making us ambivalent about the power of the latter in conditioning, for better or worse, the certainties of the former. This has resurrected and reinforced additional dichotomies: "developed" and "developing" world, and so forth. We speak not merely of the global rich and poor, but also politically of the "multilateral" and interconnected as against the polarized and segmented. Recalling Lévi-Strauss's mediating structures, we might also note that multilateralism and its institutional expressions—international organizations, legal regimes, and conventions—

have been more common in the "West" than in the "East," which appears to prefer for the time being older models of world order: balance of power and empire, although the distinctions here are probably more relevant within regions than between them.

It is no accident that one of the first and most obvious symptoms of the arrival of globalization to "new" areas is a rise in chauvinism, be it nationalism, subnationalism, regionalism, or some other variation. These do not result neatly from simple hatred or fear; they are not strictly "antiglobal." They are more likely to come as a reaction to the ambivalence of globalization, from a desire to enjoy its benefits without paying its costs, and as a step away from its essential unfamiliarity—Bauman's "horror of indetermination." Strangers are scarier than enemies; threats captivate us more than risks. As such, our responses suggest a form of global self-hatred whose only remedies seem to be an acceptance of the world as it is or a total renunciation of it.

\*

Sadly, the first course has not been followed by everyone, which has led to some terrible results for the rest of us. Indeed, the consequences of ambivalence are most dire in matters of war and peace. Millions are affected. Mixed signals often bring about crises and then wars, or prolong those wars that have already begun, among the most vicious being civil wars—a case of ambivalence run amok. The historian Michael Howard used to state a rule about intervening in civil wars: "Don't do it." But if you must do it, he said, be sure to pick one side and stick with it. And be sure it's the side most likely to win. This rule is often violated by well- and not-so-well-meaning outsiders, as in Afghanistan throughout the 1990s, where an interminable civil war was perpetuated by so many outside powers that the lines between civil and "proxy" became impossible to draw, not only within Afghanistan but across the nation's borders as well, where all of its neighbors found, in the fragile ethnic and other balancing acts taking place on their own territories, motives for perpetual intervention. Gains by any side or faction brought countergains and concomitant losses by others "at home" and "next door" with regular, almost mechanical predictability. Such is the paradox of the buffer state, as German geo-politicians once described it, inasmuch as it plays the simultaneous roles of magnet and segregator of armed conflict. Today's experts call this situation an "internationalized civil war," which, if you think about it, makes no sense at all except in the realm of pure am-bivalence where state borders are matters of life and death, and also meaningless.

Since the second half of the twentieth century there have been few outright military victories. Even Pyrrhic victories have been rare, apart from those in the Middle East, which are interesting exceptions but also full of ambivalence in certain ways. Warring parties have tended to pause rather than fight to the end. Many such conflicts, in spite of unique differences, are prolonged by their profitability to one or more of the major warring parties or a similar motive on the part of external actors who intervene there. And when such outsiders make the conflict their own—as America did in Vietnam, for example—the ambivalence is magnified, or multiplied as the case may be, by the mood of the "home front," by the characteristic impatience of interventionists, by contending, often contradictory, "doctrines" ("deterrence" versus "containment," in the Vietnam case), and most of all by the disparities in the scope and nature of the war for those doing the fighting and for those boosting or resisting it from the outside. The more outsiders seek to limit their liability, the harder it becomes for them to prevail, no matter how powerful they are, and, paradoxically, the longer the conflict lasts. The classic guerrilla formula of translating weakness into strength is not intrinsically ambivalent, but the effects—*pace* Bauman's units in their dark alleys—often are. These end up being wars you can't win or lose.

Just as wars once settled—or put a temporary end to—the ambivalent condition of peace, so now do "peace processes" blur the perceptible certainty of war. The notion of victory has subsided in favor of something else, something in between, a quasi-armistice or stalled, "frozen conflict." They exist on nearly every continent. Peace is no longer the absence of war nor is war the absence of peace; peace has become a process, an aspirational state of mind, as Antony Adolf has described it, rather than an objective condition. Peace may still be the norm (there is, strictly speaking, more peace than war in the world, despite the latter's horrors); but peace is no longer Sir Henry Maine's "invention," no longer a distinctive category with its own inherent logic; it is instead something else, a state of betweenness, an intermediate place in constant disputation. This may be because power itself seems to have evolved into something more latent, or potential, than in the past.

The absence of a clear line between war and peace is familiar. The prevalence of that line was an important aspect of modernity, ironic in that modernity also gave us total war, the war to end all wars, permanent war for permanent peace, and the Cold War— the protracted *Sitzkrieg*. We speak here not of ambiguity per se, but again of ambivalence— of living in *both* a state of war and a state of peace, of not being able to separate them, as the two have so interpenetrated as to have become existentially interdependent.

The challenge for politics and statecraft is to fashion a position of resolve without denying, exploiting, or perverting our inner condition of ambivalence. For no matter how much we feel that making a clear choice, even the wrong choice, and putting our best energies behind it is always better than vacillating, ambivalence may in the end get the better of us. "For to lay siege to the problem of ambivalence," wrote Robert Merton, "need not mean to conquer it." So long as we embrace, or at least accept, ambivalence as individuals, we may continue to decry and contain it constructively as a society.

Perhaps doing so can usher in a new era of human progress; or perhaps not.

# Acknowledgments

## ACKNOWLEDGMENTS

The author is grateful to Matthew Abbate, Sissela Bok, Roger Conover, Neva Goodwin, Yasuyo Iguchi, Akira Iriye, Bruce Mazlish, and Yi-Fu Tuan for their thoughtfulness and generosity; and to Col. Sam Gardiner, USAF (Ret.), whose war games introduced him to the many dangers of ambivalence.

# References

Adolf, Antony. *Peace: A World History*. Cambridge, UK: Polity Press, 2009.

Bauman, Zygmunt. *Modernity and Ambivalence*. Cambridge, UK: Polity Press, 1991.

Bauman, Zygmunt. "Modernity and Clarity: The Story of a Failed Romance." In Heinz Otto Luthe and Rainer E. Wiedenmann, eds., *Ambivalenz. Studien zum kulturtheoretischen und empirischen Gehalt einer Kategorie der Erschliessung des Unbestimmten*. Opladen: Leske & Budrich, 1997.

Bell, Clive. *Civilization*. 1928; West Drayton, UK: Penguin Books, 1947.

Berger, Peter L., and Anton C. Zijderveld. *In Praise of Doubt: How to Have Convictions Without Becoming a Fanatic*. New York: HarperCollins, 2009.

Bierce, Ambrose. *The Devil's Dictionary*, s.vv. "Indecision" and "Truth." Vol. 7 of *The Collected Works of Ambrose Bierce*. New York and Washington: Neale Publishing Company, 1911.

Empson, William. *Seven Types of Ambiguity*. London: Chatto and Windus, 1930.

Fitzgerald, F. Scott. "The Crack-Up." *Esquire*, February 1936. Rpt. in Fitzgerald, *The Crack-Up*, ed. Edmund Wilson. New York: J. Laughlin, 1945.

Hobsbawm, Eric. *Age of Extremes: The Short Twentieth Century, 1914–1991*. London: Michael Joseph, 1994.

Howard, Michael. *The Invention of Peace: Reflections on War and International Order.* New Haven: Yale University Press, 2000.

Koselleck, Reinhart. *Futures Past: On the Semantics of Historical Time.* Trans. Keith Tribe. Cambridge, MA: MIT Press, 1985.

Langer, Susanne K. *Mind: An Essay on Human Feeling.* Baltimore: Johns Hopkins University Press, 1967.

Lears, T. J. Jackson. *No Place of Grace: Antimodernism and the Transformation of American Culture, 1880–1920.* New York: Pantheon Books, 1981.

Margalit, Avishai. *On Compromise and Rotten Compromises.* Princeton: Princeton University Press, 2010.

Meerloo, Joost A. M. *The Two Faces of Man.* New York: International Universities Press, 1954.

Merton, Robert K. *Sociological Ambivalence and Other Essays.* New York: Free Press, 1976.

Orwell, George. *1984.* London: Secker and Warburg, 1949.

"Palinurus" (Cyril Connolly). *The Unquiet Grave: A Word Cycle.* 1944; New York: Persea Books, 1981.

Sagan, Carl. *The Dragons of Eden: Speculations on the Evolution of Human Intelligence*. New York: Random House, 1977.

Schelling, Thomas C. *Choice and Consequence*. Cambridge, MA: Harvard University Press, 1984.

Wahrman, Dror. *The Making of the Modern Self: Identity and Culture in Eighteenth-Century England*. New Haven: Yale University Press, 2004.

# ON AMBIVALENCE

The Problems and Pleasures of
Having It Both Ways

Kenneth Weisbrode

Why is it so hard to make up our minds? Adam
and Eve set the template: Do we or don't we eat the
apple? They chose, and nothing was ever the same
again. With this book, Kenneth Weisbrode offers a
crisp, literate, and provocative introduction to the
age-old struggle with ambivalence.

Ambivalence results from a basic desire to have it
both ways. This is only natural—although insisting
upon it against all reason often results not in "both"
but in the disappointing "neither." Ambivalence
has insinuated itself into our culture as a kind of
obligatory reflex, or default position, before practi-
cally every choice we make. It affects not only individuals. Organizations, societies, and cultures can
also be ambivalent. How often have we asked the
scornful question, "Are we the Hamlet of nations?"

How often have we demanded that our leaders appear decisive, judicious, and stalwart? And how eager have we been to censure them when they hesitate or waver?

Weisbrode traces the concept of ambivalence, from the Garden of Eden to Freud and beyond. The Obama era, he says, may be America's own era of ambivalence: neither red nor blue but a multicolored kaleidoscope. Ambivalence, he argues, need not be destructive. We must learn to distinguish it from its symptoms—selfishness, ambiguity, and indecision—and accept that frustration, guilt, and paralysis felt by individuals need not lead automatically to a collective pathology.

Drawing upon examples from philosophy, history, literature, and the social sciences, *On Ambivalence* is a pocket-sized portrait of a complex human condition. It should be read by anyone who has ever grappled with making the right choice.

KENNETH WEISBRODE is a writer living in Ankara, Turkey. He is the author of *The Atlantic Century*.

"Ambivalence haunts individuals and societies, intensifying as the world moves toward global modernity. What a relief and a pleasure, then, to be able to recommend, without ambivalence, this elegant meditation on ambivalence."

—Yi-Fu Tuan, University of Wisconsin–Madison